Peaceful Garden

CreativeColoringBooksForAdults.com

MandaLove Press

www.CreativeColoringBooksForAdults.com

https://www.facebook.com/CreativeColoringBooks

Published by MandaLove Press, LLC

First Edition Printed August 2015

ISBN-13: 978-0692516829

ISBN-10: 0692516824

Printed in the United States of America

Distributed by Adult Coloring Book Creative

Life began in a garden …

Take a walk through 50 garden-creature inspired mandala patterns and fall in love with the art of coloring. These fanciful designs are filled with delightful garden imagery and will appeal to your imagination by offering hours of relaxation and coloring fun. Unwind in the whimsy!

Get ready for hours of creative fun for the kids and quiet time for you.

These mandala designs are printed one to a page, but markers can bleed through even the best paper. Two blotter pages have been added to the back of the book for you to use to keep your artwork pristine.

Free Coloring Pages …

Subscribe to our newsletter today and we'll send you a free mandala to color. You'll also have a chance to win a brand new coloring book! We choose a new winner every month: http://CreativeColoringBooksForAdults.SubscribeMeNow.com/

Join us on Facebook and you'll have access to free coloring pages and more chances to win free coloring supplies and coloring books: https://www.Facebook.com/CreativeColoringBooks

Look for our coloring books on Amazon and at your local bookstore!

Thank you for supporting independent artists.

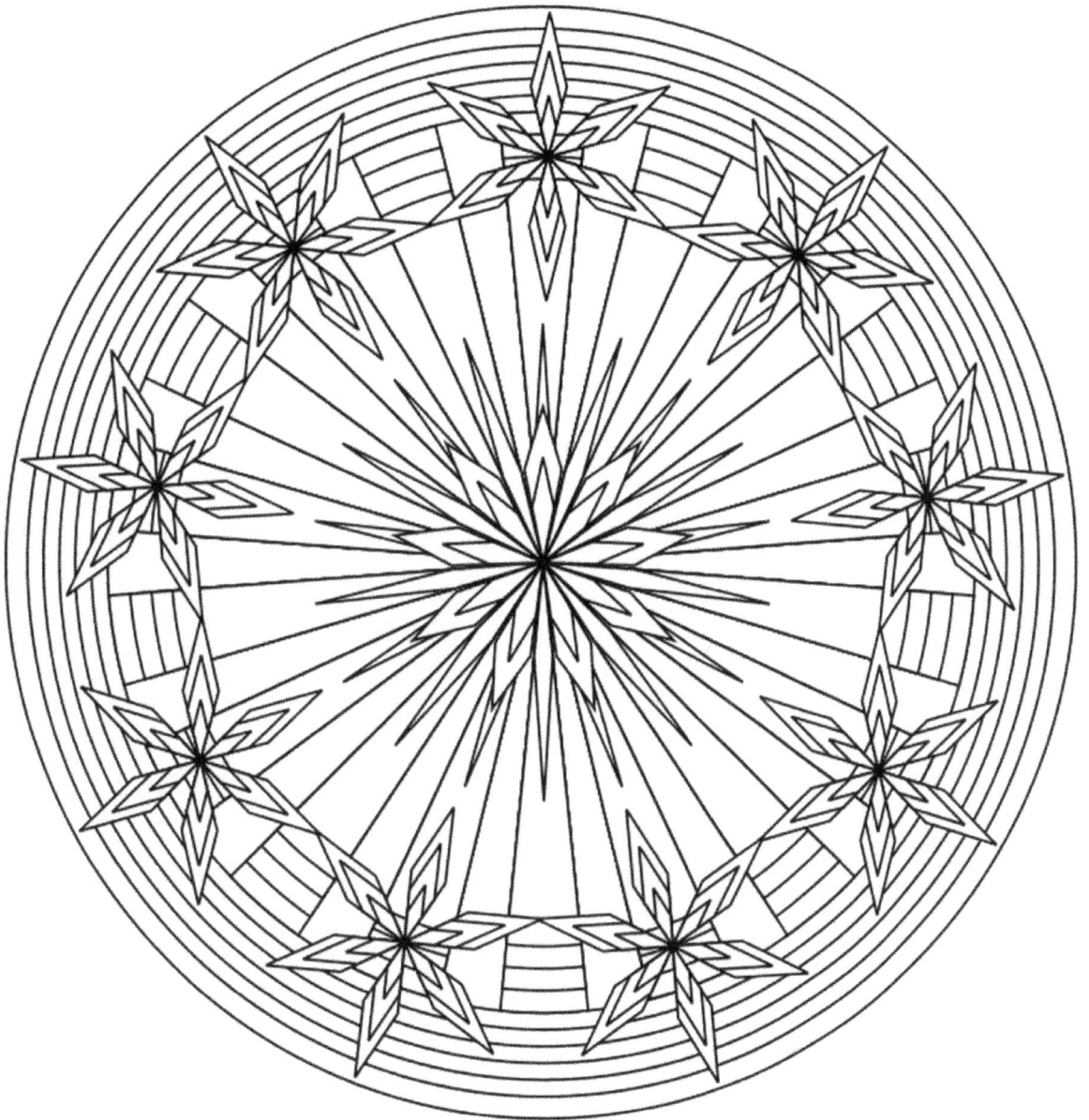

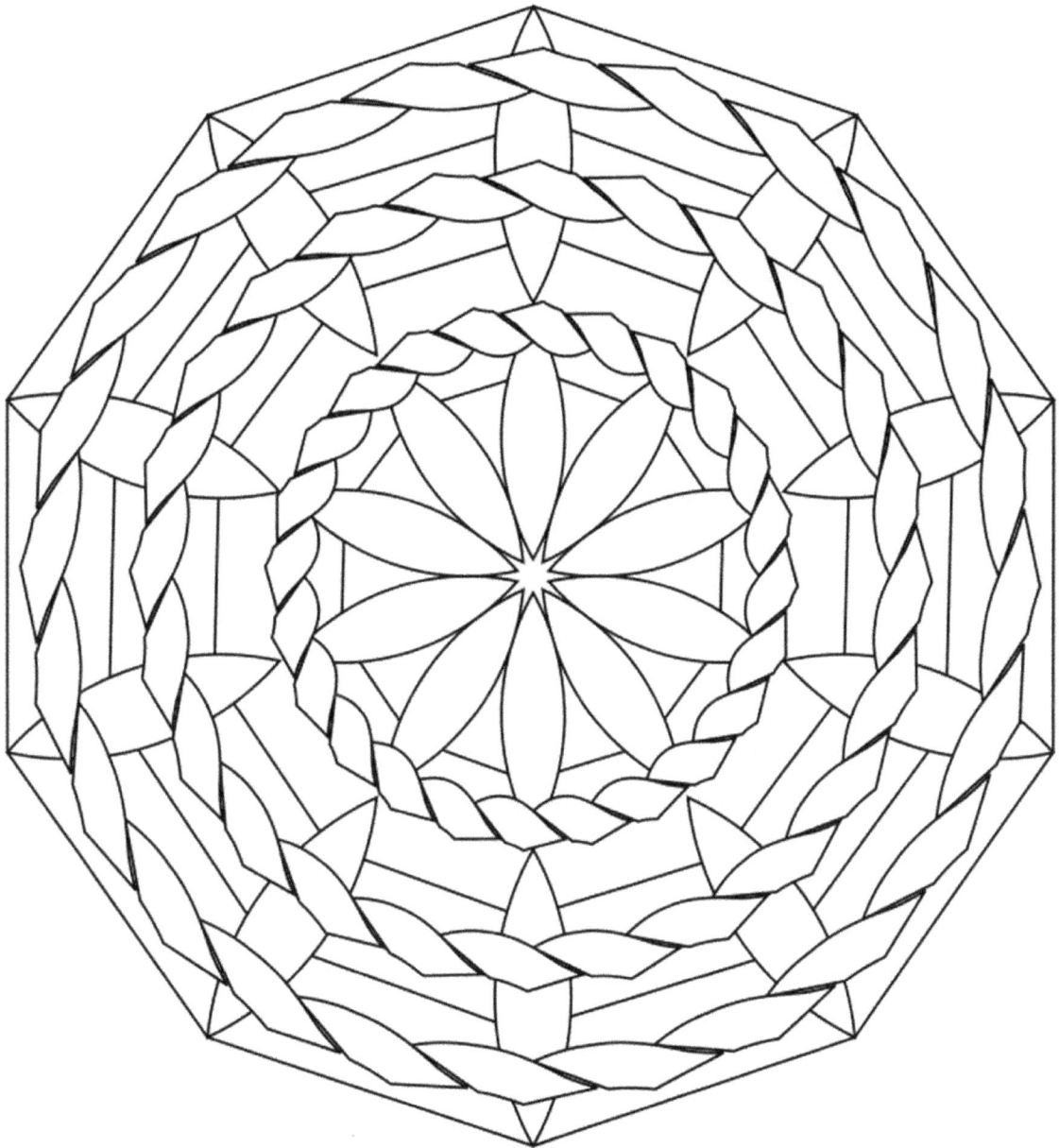

Notes

Notes

Blotter Page

Two blotter pages have been included for your convenience. Remove one or both and use them as a barrier between the page you are coloring and the next. The designs in this book have been printed on one side of the page, but markers often bleed through even the best paper. To keep your art work pristine as you color and create, use another piece of paper as a buffer between the pages of this book, or use a thin piece of cardboard (cut one side from a cereal box, or use the thin cardboard insert that is found inside a new shirt)

Blotter Page

Two blotter pages have been included for your convenience. Remove one or both and use them as a barrier between the page you are coloring and the next. The designs in this book have been printed on one side of the page, but markers often bleed through even the best paper. To keep your art work pristine as you color and create, use another piece of paper as a buffer between the pages of this book, or use a thin piece of cardboard (cut one side from a cereal box, or use the thin cardboard insert that is found inside a new shirt)

www.ingramcontent.com/pod-product-compliance
Lightning Source LLC
Chambersburg PA
CBHW081214020426
42331CB00012B/3030